MONEY
MINDSET

MONEY MINDSET

Wealth Building Roadmap for Network Marketers

Brian Carruthers

MONEY MINDSET

Copyright © 2015 by Brian Carruthers

Published by Next Century Publishing
www.nextcenturypublishing.com

Editing and layout by Paul Braoudakis

www.fostermentor.com

ISBN: 978-1-68102-148-5
Library of Congress Control Number: 2015950203

Printed in the United States of America

NEXT CENTURY
PUBLISHING

CONTENTS

ACKNOWLEDGMENTS

There are two ways we can learn how to build wealth — by having great, wealthy mentors willing to teach us what they have learned, or by learning through trial and error on our own. Many people do not seek mentorship, but rather choose to travel the financial journey on their own and pray for the best. I knew from an early age it is best to seek help from those who have what you want. So I must thank the mentors in my life, both personal and from afar. Nobody came knocking on my door to force their advice on me. I went knocking, and a few mentors opened their doors to me. I went into my learning with a very open mind, and I made sure to apply everything I could.

Thank you to my parents for being such amazing role models for being smart with their money. Growing up as a child, I watched them build large businesses and amass great fortunes. Although we had everything we needed and wanted, they were also quite frugal. I learned so much from them about how to treat and respect money. The legacy they will leave behind is far greater than bank accounts and assets. They passed on a legacy of a wealth mindset. It is extremely important for me to live in the same way, and in turn pass on that mindset to my own family. My son and unborn children will be the beneficiaries of all that I have learned.

To Paul J Meyer, who spent personal time with me, helped me to think bigger about building wealth and making my work my ministry. I learned that my mission cannot be just about my own financial goals, but should include helping many others to change their lives, too. To whom much is given, much is expected. My mission in life is to empower people financially, and to pass along to the willing the principles and strategies I have learned.

To my fellow network marketers, I urge you to slow down to speed up. Take the time to develop the right foundation of sound financial philosophies before running out there to conquer the world. Build your empires on solid ground so that no tremble can bring you down. All the money in the world will do you no good if you are loading it into a box riddled with holes. Your money mindset should be your foremost concern. Let me help you the way some of my mentors helped me. Take me with you, and always refer back to the mindset in this book to guide your financial decisions. I look forward to seeing you build your wealth bigger than you have ever imagined possible.

INTRODUCTION

I fell in love with the network marketing industry and saw how this business model can change lives. I saw people use leverage and create incomes they had never seen before. It was revolutionary! But as time went on, I saw things that bothered me to my core. I felt the pain when I saw friends in the industry who were mismanaging their newfound money. I saw them blowing money like there was some guarantee that their income would always grow and flow forever. New cars, new homes, new clothes, wristwatches, first class flying, fancy vacations, and all types of other splurges became their world.

But this wild horse nature of unbridled spending behavior almost always caught up to them. Their spending continued to outpace their earnings and, though they had money, they were just broke at a higher level. Or something would happen beyond their control and they were caught unprepared. Perhaps the company they were building in had problems, or some team members left and they lost sales volume, or the economy had taken a bad turn. The next thing you know, their income is cut in half. They were losing their cars and homes. They were behind on paying taxes. In effect, their lives were flipped upside down.

Why did this happen? In a word (or two): *Wrong mindset.* This scenario is indicative of what happens when people find a way to make money, but they don't have the right mindset or plan to deal with the money they are making. I feel the joy deep inside of me when I see a network marketer achieving success, as that huge smile goes across their face from ear to ear. I love knowing that their financial stress is being relieved, and that they are living a richer life than they ever knew before. But on the flip side, when things turn, I feel the pain inside knowing how this shocking surprise rocks their world.

This is why I had to write this book.

My first book, *Making My First Ten Million*, was written to help attract people into the business. My second book, *Building an Empire*, was written to teach how to actually build the business from scratch to significant income in network marketing. And I am excited that those two books have been wildly successful in accomplishing those two goals. But now that we have so many people making incredible incomes, I feel an obligation to talk about how to be smart with your money.

Now there may be critics who might knock this book for not being a detailed 300-page tome on stock investing, or a thorough treatise on tax accounting for home-based business owners.

But please hear me, that is *not* what this book is about. This book is about *mindset*. It is about thinking differently regarding money and wealth, so that you will have an inflamed desire to pursue further knowledge on all such subjects. I can tell you that what I write about here is exactly what has served me in my life very, very well. While I am not a CPA, certified financial planner, or even an expert stock investor, the principles you are about to absorb have created a level of wealth that provides a great level of financial peace and security in my life.

Let's begin the conversation assuming that many readers are currently in debt, and just beginning to figure out a plan to gain financial independence. Of course, I expect that some readers might already have a great plan and are further along in their quest to build wealth. Frankly, since a wise person is never done learning, maybe some readers are further along than I am. But in any case, if you are reading this, it means you want to do better. You want every advantage you can stack in your favor.

MINDSET BONUS

Listen in on sporadic live conference calls to get further instruction and investment updates from Brian. Simply register your email address at *moneymindsetbook.com* right now. The next call may be coming up soon!

So here we go.

THE MONEY MINDSET

Money is a very, very powerful thing. It is a force that moves the world. People will work all day for it, steal and cheat for it, lie awake at night because they don't have enough of it, and change others' lives by giving it away. Many people live their lives subjected as a slave to money, while others are the masters of money. If you want to be a master of money, you must first develop an understanding of money, a respect for it, and an appreciation of it.

Understand it. Respect/appreciate it. Attract it. Make it. Keep it. Control it. Grow it. Impact others with it.

Before we can truly delve into developing our money mindset, it makes sense to try and define what mindset is really all about. There are several "official" definitions of mindset, ranging from Webster's *"A mental inclination, tendency, or habit,"* to Oxford's *"The established set of attitudes held by someone."*

There are several others as well, but all you really need to understand are two things: 1) A mindset is *a way of thinking*, and 2) Mindset *really* matters.

According to Carol S. Dweck, the author of *Mindset: The New Psychology of Success: How We Can Learn to Fulfill Our Potential,* there are two different kinds of mindsets — a *fixed* mindset and a *growth* mindset. On her website, she defines both.

> *In a **fixed mindset,** people believe their basic qualities, like their intelligence or talent, are simply fixed traits. They spend their time documenting their intelligence or talent instead of developing them. They also believe that talent alone creates success — without effort. They're wrong.*

> *In a **growth mindset**, people believe that their most basic abilities can be developed through dedication and hard work — brains and talent are just the starting point. This view creates a love of learning and a resilience that is essential for great accomplishment. Virtually all great people have had these qualities.*

Needless to say, we will focus heavily in this book on the *growth mindset* since we are trying to grow our ourselves, our incomes, and our businesses to greater levels. Throughout the journey of this book, we will assess your current philosophies about money (your fixed mindset) and take you through a transformation so you end up in a place where money just seems to find its way to you for the rest of your life (your growth mindset).

Who we are is what we attract. Get ready for some mental shifts.

How Did We Get Here?

It is important to know that you will not transform your financial situation overnight. Where you are financially today is the aggregate result of the decisions you have made over the last 5-10 years of your life — decisions driven by your philosophies and your relationship with money. As famed author and business coach Jim Rohn taught, "You can change your life in any five years. From age 35 to 40, age 23 to 28, age 59 to 64." Just as you should not expect to get rich quick overnight, you also should not expect to become a financial wizard overnight, either.

But the fact that you are reading this book sets you apart from and ahead of 90 percent of the population.

Even small changes in your mindset and actions, done consistently over an extended period of time, can transform you. Darren Hardy of *Success* magazine calls it "The Compound Effect." You are either making the correct little decisions every day, or you are making little judgment errors that, compounded over time, will make or break you. In life and in finances, you either exercise self-discipline, or the world will discipline you. Either way, you will be disciplined. So the point is to set your expectations properly. Expect that this will be a journey ... but one that is worth it if you value getting wealthy.

If you were to study *wealthy* people and study *poor* people like I have, you will find that they are very different. But to find out why, we must look beneath the difference in their bank accounts, the cars they drive, or their spending habits. These are all merely symptoms of their mindsets and philosophies about money. How people feel about money, and even how they feel about whether they are deserving of abundance in their lives, will dictate whether they will attract wealth or repel it. Poor people mostly feel they are undeserving, and that money is not good. They sometimes even despise those who have created wealth. They will claim that money is not important, all the while they live with high levels of stress because they do not have the financial resources to afford the cost of living. After years of living with this philosophy, they become accustomed to a life of lack and oppression.

Broke is different than poor. Broke is temporary. I have studied many people who had the right mindset and philosophies, but they were working on their wealth or in between winning streaks. Just because their bank account was at zero, that didn't mean they were poor. They had the wealthy mind-set, and were working on attracting and creating the results. Donald Trump was worth over a *billion* dollars. But for years during a real estate downturn, his business ventures were hit hard and he found himself in personal debt over $900 million. People complain about having no money all the time, but can you imagine being below the water line by $900 million? But Donald Trump was never poor. Poor is a state of mind, and he always had the *wealth mindset* even when he was down. And it was his mindset (and work ethic and skills) that saw him back to the top — to the tune of his current $4 billion net worth, according to *Forbes* magazine. Because he was never poor, he became *unbroke*.

Stay the Course

I ask up front that you stay with me as we take this journey together. You may desire to run ahead if you feel like you are reading something that you already know. But I submit to you that you cannot get the desired result if you decide to skip parts of this wealth mindset building process. *How* to make the money and *what* to do with the money — these are the easier components to learn. But you do not want to build your financial structure on sand. So we must drill really deep and lay an extremely solid foundation first. The deeper the foundation, the bigger your financial empire can be built upon it. The good news is you've already found the *how*: Through this incredible business model we call network marketing. You discovered the better way to get ahead financially, and have committed to this path (at least part time) to creating wealth and freedom. I have watched many thousands of people choose this vehicle to be their income-producing machine as they exited the rat race of living check to check and chasing money indefinitely.

Think about what attracted you to this business. You likely saw the ability to get paid for making sales, but quickly realized that the most powerful kind of money comes in the form of passive overrides on the sales made by others *and* the lifetime residual income stream from your customer base. This is where the vision of most network marketers ends. They make money and they spend it just as quickly. Now that you have this new source of income, it is vital that you have specific plans for what to do with it so you arrive where you desire in the next five years.

Let's get your mind thinking about going to the next level. You've heard the sayings, "It takes money to make money," and, "The rich keep getting richer." These statements do hold truths, but only for the educated and disciplined. Your network marketing business is the cash machine. You must have the intent to build wealth instead of spending your money. You must learn how to legally keep as much of what you earn as you can. Then the ultimate goal is to learn how to invest; how to put overalls on your money and have it go to work for you. The end game should be for you to be able to live your life off the interest income from your investments without ever touching the principle. For example, my goal was to create enough cash flow from my network marketing business to invest $10 million, which at just 5 percent interest, would generate $500,000 a year for me to live on — without ever having to touch the $10 million. Can you imagine?

Most people want to jump right into asking about what investments they should put their monies into. That is not the right question ... yet. We first must establish the right mindset. Without this as a foundation, you can never get to the destination of financial freedom. Sadly, 95 percent of the population does not have this mindset. Once your thinking about money is right, then we can get into how to keep the money that you earn. This will address your spending habits, as well as business expenses and paying taxes. Next we can determine some strategies for investing what you have kept, so you can watch your money compound and grow. Lastly — in the end this is what matters most — you can find ways to use your wealth to help others and change the world.

The Love of Money ...

The first place to start is to examine your personal relationship with money. How do you consciously think about money? And even deeper, how were you conditioned and programmed to *feel* about money throughout your life? Many people have never stopped to ask themselves these important questions.

Ask yourself if you've ever heard these statements:

"The love of money is the root of all evil."
"Money can't buy you happiness."
"Rich people take advantage of others."
"It's not good to be greedy, so money is not important."
"The love of money is bad."

If you were raised in an environment where you heard such things, you are likely *repelling* money from you instead of *attracting* it to you — and you don't even realize it. Think about it. If your subconscious self deems money to be intrinsically bad or evil, it will not want you to have it. Consciously, however, in the real world of bills and expenses, you know you need money to live. You have likely worked hard, almost as a slave to money, all of your life. You never really thought of money as a good thing, but rather a necessary evil in life.

When your mind deems something as "evil," it tends to repel it. For instance, if you ingest contaminated food or something that is poisonous, your conscious mind does not even have to be triggered. An unconscious message is sent to your body to throw it up, to rid your body of that which is bad or could hurt you. In the same way, your environment has wired or programmed you to act in this same way with regard to money. If money is bad or evil, you will unconsciously want to get rid of it as fast as you earn it. Thus, it is next to impossible for you to ever grow your wealth.

Another example of how a physical disdain for money can manifest in your relationship with money can be found in a recent study, "How 'Dirty' Money Affects Spending Behavior." In a paper titled "Money Isn't Everything, But it Helps if it Doesn't Look Used: How the Physical Appearance of Money Influences Spending," professor Theodore Noseworthy called it the "Ick Factor."

"We tend not to like money that looks like a lot of others have touched it," Noseworthy says. "People want to get rid of worn currency because they're disgusted by the contamination of others." He adds, "Where someone with a crisp bill would tend to hold onto it … someone with a worn bill tends to use it as soon as they get it."

So whether it's your brain expelling poison from your body to keep you healthy, or your getting rid of dirty money due to subconscious disgust, these are very strong parallels to your own personal relationship with money. Take a moment now to evaluate your money mindset. If you have always had trouble attracting money, or keeping what you have earned, I am confident you will remember hearing the negative programming about money earlier in your life. The good news is that you can reprogram your mind starting now. You can attract money into your life. To do this, you must swing to the other side of the spectrum. You can learn to *love* money.

Read this aloud right now: **"I LOVE MONEY!"**

How did that feel? Did that cause you to feel uneasy? Would you be afraid that people might judge you if they heard you say this? How would your friends or family label you for saying this? Does this fear maybe keep you from gaining wealth? It is important for each of us to recognize that we all seek acceptance, love, and respect from others. If others think of money as evil, of course we wouldn't want to speak against their moral truths. So how do we deal with this? We must create our own new truths. Then we can better deal with the outside world that would rather have us join them in the comfortable state of lack.

You see, I love money. I really do. And because I love it, I seek it and I attract it. But let me explain how I think and what my mindset is all about. Money is not paper nor piles of gold. Money is a means of exchange of value, a means to an end. So when I say, "I love money," what I am really saying is "I love what money can do." Money is not bad or good, in and of itself. The greed of it, or doing bad things for or with money is where bad can creep in. More money will simply make you more of what you already are. If you were a jerk before you had money, you'll just be a richer jerk. Money won't make you a better person. Conversely, if you were a good and giving person *before* you had money, you'll be an even better and more giving person now that you have it.

Here are a few questions to help you learn to love money and what it can do.

- Assume someone in your family became very ill and she needed advanced medical care to save her life. But this treatment was only available overseas and the cost was going to be into the hundreds of thousands. How much would you love to pull out your checkbook and handle it altogether? Would you love it?

- Your son wants to go to a private school in town because they offer the best programs for his interests. But tuition for this school is more than $20,000 a year. How great would it feel to go into his bedroom one night and say, "Honey, we are going to let you go to the school of your dreams"? Wouldn't you *love* that?

- Every Sunday, your church shows how much it's trying to raise to fulfill the budget for mission trips and community outreach programs for those in need. You see that the budget is behind by $22,000. Wouldn't you love to be able to drop in on the pastor on Monday and hand him a check for that amount with a big smile on your heart? Wouldn't you *love* that?

- Your parents haven't driven a new car in almost 15 years. Times are tight, and the car just isn't what you want them to be driving. How amazing would it feel to have them walk out of their front door one day to find a gorgeous new car parked in their driveway with a huge red bow across the hood, and "I love you Mom and Dad!" written across the windshield? Wouldn't you *love* that?

- The economy dives into recession. Jobs are being lost, and people can't afford to keep their homes. The stock market is crashing and people's 401Ks are cut in half overnight. Wouldn't you *love* the peace of mind that comes from knowing you created a financial moat around you and your family that can endure even such a deep economic downturn?

Can you find all sorts of things to fall in love with based on what money can do for you? I decided early in life to attach in my mind the goodness in these things with the concept of money itself. These things that I love have caused me to *want* money. We attract that which we want and think about. If I love the things and blessings I can bestow, I can love that which will make these things possible. I didn't start off enjoying reading books. It was quite tiring to me. I would fall asleep after reading 20 pages, or have to go back and re-read an entire page again because I didn't absorb what I had just read. But I *loved what I got from* reading, so now I tell people I love reading.

With this understanding, repeat aloud once again: "I LOVE MONEY!"

How did that feel this time? I expect this new psychological underpinning of these words will make you *feel* differently about them. The more you say them to yourself, and think deeply beneath the surface, the better your relationship with money will become. You attract what you think about most often. So think good thoughts about money going forward, and think often. Money is something your unconscious thoughts can help you *magnetize.*

THE WEALTH BUILDING MINDSET

Wealth is a noun, while *rich* is an adjective. If someone says, "I am rich," this means their life is filled with blessings or trappings of success. It is wonderful for someone to want to become rich, as long as it does not cloud their value system or the vision of who they are. Wealth is a thing — a measurement of time. Wealth is the length of time you can sustain your accustomed standard of living (expenses) without needing to acquire more money to pay for it.

For example, if your monthly cost of living is $5,000 a month, and you have $100,000 in the bank, then your wealth is 20 months. This means that you could continue living your life with no new income for 20 months before your well runs dry. Would you feel wealthy in this scenario? Probably not. Heaven forbid you lose your job tomorrow and you could not find work. You would be out on the street in less than two years.

That fear would cause a person not to feel secure. And security is an important human drive. We all want it. So to me, true wealth is having enough money to live comfortably and securely for the balance of your years on earth, even without working to earn another dollar.

How Much Money Will You Need?

Have you created a budget for yourself? Do you know how much you will need to have put away to be able to retire? Forget about all the travel and the fun stuff we tell ourselves we're going to do when we retire. Let's look at just *eating*:

Let's assume you and your spouse want to retire at 65, and expect to live for 20 years. Let's say the two of you want to eat three times a day, and you want to do so all 365 days of the year. Let's calculate based on a mere $7 per meal.

Two people *x* 20 years *x* 365 days *x* three meals *x* $7 dollars = $306,600

You would need to have more than $300,000 in the bank ... just to be able to eat! This assumes you don't live longer than 20 years. This financial scenario allows no money for gas, utilities, insurance, golf, holiday presents for the grandkids, clothes, or medicines — just food! And no eating out ... that would be too expensive!

How much is in your bank account right now? Is it greater than, or less than $306,600?

If your number is far away from this estimate, we've got some work to do. The good news is, you can do it! It will take determination and focus. We will decide now to earn more, spend less, and invest more. We will get you to retirement with the wealth you need.

Network Marketers and Their Quandary

In our industry, we are drawn to the stories of people earning big money, traveling the world, driving exotic cars, and posing for the camera in front of their mansions. The flashy trappings of success are supposed to prove that this business is successful, and insinuate that they, too, can have all of this.

But we all must realize that this is a slippery slope. In many ways, it's a trap.

I have watched all too many networkers living way above their means. On the outside, they look dazzling and happy. But when they log onto their computer at night and look at their online bank statement, the smile disappears. On the inside, many are toiling, restless, and scared. Eventually this causes people to make poor decisions out of desperation, rather than smart decisions born from peace of mind and confidence. You will see networkers who cannot stay put building their business in one company long enough to gain wealth because their spending-habitualized desperation causes them to look for the next shiny object to rescue them.

The sad reality is that on any given day I can show you two different people who are currently making $50,000 a year from their network marketing business ... but in five years, one will be broke, while the other has built a sizable net worth. Sad, but true.

If you want to lose weight, you can eat less, or work out more. But if you want to get even better results faster, you can eat less *and* work out more! A similar law applies in wealth building. If you want to build wealth, you can spend less, or earn more. But if you want to get there faster, you can spend less *and* earn more!

You can't always control *how much* you earn, but even without earning more, you *can* immediately control the spending and what you do with the surplus money (more on this later). You're always going to continue to work on growing your income. But if income growth is your only focus, you may just end up earning more and still be broke at a higher level. There's nothing gained by earning $100,000 a year and spending $100,000 a year. Actually, all you'll have done is raised the bar of your expenses and skewed your wealth calculation to now have fewer years to live off your savings. So it is imperative that you get control of these first two topics right off the bat.

Spending

Live below your means. This is the easiest way to frame my advice. Whatever amount of income you have coming in, live on less than that. I cannot make it any simpler. When in doubt, just revert to that rule. Truly wealthy people live below their means. Take a look at Warren Buffett, one of the top three wealthiest people in the entire world with a $63 billion net worth. As of this writing, he is still living in the same house he bought for $31,500 in 1958. He doesn't drive a super expensive car, either. He doesn't need to impress anyone, and you can see the peace of mind and heart all over his gentle, smiling face.

Buffett once shared that success has nothing to do with the house you live in. There are many ways someone can measure or define success, but the size of your house really shouldn't have anything to do with it. While life will have its ups and downs, it's the continuous learning, thinking for yourself, developing good habits, focusing on the long term, and having fun on the journey, that will set you up for success in life.

Too often we get caught up with celebrities on television who are glorified for their mansions, exotic cars, jewelry, and jet-set lifestyle. If you let yourself idolize such people, it is inevitable that you will try to keep up with them in your own proportionate way. This is a recipe for disaster. In fact, many of these clowns often lose most or all of the money they earned because they never took the time to learn how to have a wealth-building mindset in the first place.

This is why I am so excited you are reading this book. We are going to ensure you keep the wealth you create so you can pass it on and/or bless the world around you with it.

Disposable Income — There's No Such Thing!

Let's talk about spending habits. This topic is more than just refraining from buying expensive homes and cars. It pervades our daily lives in much smaller transactions. We are talking about developing a new mindset about what things cost, and creating a mental framework for deciding whether the cost of something is worth robbing from your future wealth to pay for it.

Every dollar we spend has an "opportunity cost" attached to it. The *Rule of Seven* means that money invested at a 10 percent compounded rate of return will double every seven years. With this as a constant backdrop in your mind, think about what that $1,000 flat-screen TV really costs. Right now, it's $1,000 cash (assuming you aren't going down the debt rabbit hole and using a credit card). But had you invested that money, in seven years it would have turned into $2,000. In seven more years it would have been $4,000. So if you have a child right now who is four years old, and you hope to pay for his/her college when turning eighteen, that $1,000 TV stole $4,000 from your child's education. So the decision-making process just became different for you. A pack of gum isn't $1.50, but rather $3 ... or even $4.50!

Now I don't want to turn your life into one of miserly existence. But I do want to instill the practice of conscientious thought before you part with your hard earned money ... and even more so when your money seems to be not so hard-earned (flowing in passively from team overrides while your network marketing business is in a momentum phase).

Here is a key topic that ties right in with the opportunity cost discussion. There are many things we spend money on in our daily lives that we could choose not to buy, but rather divert those monies toward investments. Take for example, a fancy cup of coffee that costs $5. Did you need that expensive cup, or could you have brewed your own for less than a dollar? Or it could be a $6 pack of cigarettes. Or maybe even the extra premium channels on your cable TV package that add up to $70 a month or more. What if you could find just $10 a day that you could divert from spending and repurpose it into investing into your future? As these bits and pieces add up and then compound interest kicks in to grow it at 10 percent annual return, look at the following graph to see what happens.

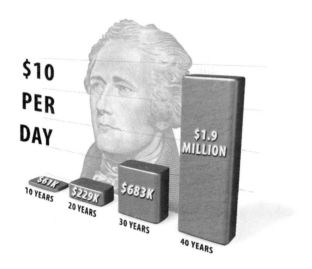

As you can see, every little bit helps. Every dollar compounds. This conversation is not even factoring in extra earnings you can invest. We are only starting with some things you currently spend money on that maybe you can cut out. It might be saying *no* to one last $12 martini at closing time. It might be flying coach rather than first class when traveling. (Even though I make millions, I still choose to fly coach for this reason. Good habits are hard to change!) Maybe you can cancel cable TV for a year and see if you really miss it. You might just become more productive as a by-product while saving money! When I say there is no such thing as "disposable income," I mean that you should intend/plan to invest every dollar you can, rather than dispose of it.

I am sensitive to the fact that in network marketing your prospects do need to see you as successful. So I do understand that we must invest in our appearance. We need to dress for success. But we need to keep that in check and not go overboard. A few nice-looking suits or dresses will do. Maybe you can reward yourself with a new outfit when you hit a benchmark goal in your business. We do want our car to be clean and modern. We do need to invest in things like dental work if needed, to ensure clean appearance and hygiene. But when people start buying things with their newfound money like a typical lottery winner, that bling-bling is the biggest telling sign that he/she will be broke when we run into them 10 years from now. I would bet on it, because the more money they make, the smarter they think they are.

Hear this clearly: Money doesn't make you smarter. As a matter of fact, I am writing this book to help people catch up with their money. After all, *money, like water, seeks its own level.* If you don't grow up to where your money is, it will come right back down to who you are. If you are used to making $30,000 a year, and your network marketing business shoots you up to $100,000, in due time you will be back to earning $30,000 if you don't develop a six-figure mindset with regard to financial literacy.

Please don't misunderstand me here. I don't want to make it sound like I'm advocating that you live like a pauper and have no quality of lifestyle. But I don't want to give you a blanket license to live a financially irresponsible life, either. So I *cau-*

tiously mention that you do need to do and have nice things. Eating out on a fun Friday night with your family or significant other, or taking a cool vacation during the year, or getting a stunning new pair of shoes ... these things can certainly happen. I am merely suggesting that you make *calculated* decisions. Later in the book we will talk about budgets, and how to set aside monies for life's pleasures. With discipline in tow, as your wealth builds, you can ratchet up the amounts you allow yourself to spend on fun.

Look, I own a Bentley GTC and a Ferrari Spyder. I am certainly all for you getting to a point when you can justify such luxuries, but ... keep it relative and *in proportion* to your income. For example, when I bought the Ferrari, it cost me *six weeks* worth of my income. To give you a frame of reference, take six weeks of your income. What kind of car could you buy with that? I got the Ferrari only after my income made it possible for me to feel good about buying it. I spend only a small percentage of my monthly income on the extras in life. I have my fixed costs like house, cars, insurance, kid's tuition, etc., but the bulk of what's left goes into investments. Let me tell you, I sleep well knowing that I have a financial moat around my family.

Why do we buy nice things? I think it's important that we contemplate this question. People spend money for things they need and things they want. It goes without saying that if we *need* something, we need something. If we need gas for our car, or heat for our home, or medicine for our health, of course that doesn't require much thought. But then we have the purchases that are driven by *want*, not need. It might be a designer purse we would love to hang on our shoulder, or the gorgeous new convertible we would love to drive around town. These purchases fill a need as well, but a different kind.

As humans, we have a *need* to feel loved, respected, and valued. We feel that people will feel more of these things about us if we are all shined up and have nice material things. It shows people we worked hard, and we made it! Quite often, part of the drive for us to work so hard is to prove to the world what we are capable of. If you wear a Rolex watch and people see it, they will know you are a success. If people see me drive my Bentley, without even getting to know me, they'll know I'm the real deal. That's how the subconscious self-conversation goes. Unfortunately, this is largely spurred on by the unrealistic media and perpetuated by our sadly materialistic society.

I'm not trying to be a Debbie Downer and say that it's all bad to buy nice things. I have many nice things, and I know who I am and that I have nothing but good intentions and values deep down inside. So I do not judge anyone for what they purchase. I merely think it merits a conversation so that we each discover why we decide to make certain purchases and how they impact us personally.

At the end of the day, we all need to decide what our value system is, and what we feel best serves us individually. Would you feel better about yourself with an $800 purse on your arm, or seeing that $800 in your bank account? Do you get more feeling of self worth from vanity or security? Both can build self-confidence, so neither answer is right or wrong. What my experience tells me from working with so many people, and discussing finances with them over the years — is that the people who spent lots of money on luxury items were not much happier if their bank accounts were still weak. Because at night when they logged in to see their bank statement, any self esteem or confidence they had came right back down to earth by the stress that comes from a lack of wealth. Money in the bank is better than spending on outwardly displays showing your success. Warren Buffett doesn't have much flash in his trappings — but he sure has the biggest flash in his confident smile! He is grounded and centered, and a great example for us all.

When in doubt, ask yourself, "Is this a *need* or a *want*?" If there is something you must spend money on because you absolutely need it, then so be it. But if the purchase is really a "want purchase," maybe you can set some business or earning goals and reward yourself with the purchase for hitting them. Let your wants drive you to be that much more disciplined and hard working. Trust me, you will enjoy so much more that which you worked tirelessly to acquire. And it's even more satisfying when it's attached to a milestone of achievement.

Debt vs. Wealth

Thoughts are things, and we always attract more of what we focus on. Don't believe it? Take a look at hypochondriacs. These are well-meaning people who continually tell themselves that they are sick. They live in a perpetual state of moans and groans and constantly tell anyone who will listen about a new ache and pain they discovered on any given day. It's easy to think that this is merely *psychological* but there's a very real *physiological* result of their flawed mindset: Their brain actually sends signals to their organs telling them that they are indeed sick. As hard as it might be to believe, they've actually *willed* themselves into a sickened state.

The same brain functions are at play here. If you focus continually on *debt* (or even getting out of debt) you will tend to attract more of it. If you focus on *wealth*, you will attract wealth. Our goal through the journey of the book is to recalibrate your thinking to focus on building wealth. It works subtly, and over time you are propelled in the direction of your thoughts.

If your goal all month long is to work hard to earn money in order to service your debts (pay bills), you'll forever be a slave to debt service. With debt on your mind, you will tend to attract more debt. But regardless of attracting more debt, let's consider what your values are. Your goal is to pay bills. So if you have $5,000 in bills, and you earn $6,000, you will pay the $5,000 to cover the bills and spend the leftover $1,000. The remaining thousand was a surplus — it was extra. So you reward yourself by going out to eat, taking a trip, buying new clothes, and finding other ways to spend it. Why not? After all, you've successfully met your goal of paying your bills, right?

Here's why this is a problem. Your focus could have been on *creating wealth* instead of servicing debt. It's a crucial shift in your mindset. It's a difference in your values. Do you need to spend money on things of today or is becoming wealthy more important?

Here is a different way to think. Your goal all month long is to *grow your wealth.* You have $5,000 in bills, and you earn $6,000. The bills do get paid, but the remaining $1,000 is already earmarked to go into your wealth/investment account. You worked all month long to make enough money to have the extra that will increase your net worth. Always remember — a growing bank account will make you feel so much better about yourself than a fancy Rolex watch or expensive new shoes or handbags.

This is the crucial decision-making you must master. What are you working for? Debt or wealth? When you have the extra $1,000, where is it going? The choice is yours. And so are the consequences.

What is more important to you?

SHOES
TRIPS ◄──── versus ────► WEALTH
TOYS FUTURE
SECURITY

Your Wealth Account

The very first thing you must do right now (if you have not done this already) is to go open a new bank account that we will call your *Wealth Account*. This will be your doorway to a wealthy future. You want to be looking at this account balance monthly, or even weekly or daily. This account always needs to be growing! This is not your rainy day fund for emergencies like a car repair, hot water heater replacement, or dental emergency. Those living expenses come out of your main working bank account you already have. This Wealth Account is not to be extracted from, but needs to be a one-way door for your money into your investment life. The only reason for money to come out is if it is being directed into a selected investment.

Remember, the goal is to take your focus off your debt and laser in on wealth creation. Set up your bills to be paid automatically from your checking account, so that you do not have to see them often. In your mind, you will now live in a world of abundance. You are leaving behind the world of lack or scarcity. Your head no longer occupies that space. You are now cutting unnecessary spending and growing your earnings to double the pace of your wealth's growth. It is exciting to mentally be living in this new realm!

You now have two income sources — one is your W-2 employee paycheck or maybe your profits from a traditional business. Your second source is your network marketing business.

Here is one way to approach your finances with these two powerful economic engines. If you are building a part-time network marketing business while working a full time job, then live off your W-2 income with the surplus (after bills) going to the Wealth Account. Then invest *all* of the proceeds from your network marketing business into your Wealth Account.

If you are already working full-time in network marketing as your sole source of income, then you will need to determine how to approach servicing your debt while maintaining the priority of building your wealth. Again, the bills get paid, taxes put aside, and the rest you save/invest.

Pay Yourself First

One of the most important wealth strategies you can employ is to pay yourself first. This means that before anyone you owe touches any of your incoming cash flow, you remember who is the number one priority. That's *you*, your family, and your future!

I learned from my mentor, Paul J Meyer, many years ago that before the money comes into your hand, you must already have a design for where it goes next. First, you have a set percentage right off the top that goes to you (your Wealth Account). In the beginning, this should be 10 percent. If you make $1,500/month, put away $150 of it. If you make $3,000/month, put away $300. As your income grows, you grow this percentage because your cost of living should not increase at the same rate of your earnings growth.

For example, if you make $12,000/month, don't just stick to paying yourself $1,200. You don't need to elevate your cost of living to $10,800/month. You can easily live on $9,000 and put away $3,000, or live on $6,000 and invest $6,000. To see what this will do for your wealth accumulation, look at the following chart. It's similar to the previous accumulation chart, but this one shows the *repeated* efforts of your daily choices and how they compound over a variety of time spans.

Based on a 10% annual rate of return

	10 years	20 years	30 years	40 years
$5 day ($150/month)	$30,982	$114,854	$341,898	$956,517
$10 day ($300/month)	$61,965	$229,709	$683,797	$1,913,034
$20 day ($600/month)	$123,931	$459,418	$1,367,595	$3,826,068
$50 day ($1,500/month)	$309,828	$1,148,545	$3,418,987	$9,565,170
$100 day ($3,000/month)	$619,656	$2,297,090	$6,837,975	$19,130,340

It is vitally important that you make your wealth building *automatic*. If you have to think about it every time you get paid, and have to consciously decide whether or not you want to pay yourself first and invest, you won't do it. You will keep putting it off. It is human nature. So you must *go right away* with urgency to your boss and ask that he/she take 10 percent of every paycheck and automatically transfer it into your new (separate) Wealth Account. Many employers can do this for you.

What if you are self-employed like me as a full-time network marketer? If your company cannot deduct from your commissions checks before sending them to you, then you can set an automatic transfer with your bank to withdraw this 10 percent right out of your main checking or savings account. Many banks do this, so check around. By making this automatic, you eliminate the possibility that your *will power* might fall short and that you'll decide to spend the money elsewhere.

Give Some of it Away

Paul Meyer also insisted you carve a second 10 percent off the top to give away. Whether supporting a church or a charity, Paul taught me that all of what I have is God's by right of creation, and that I should do good things with some of what comes in. What he found in his life was that the more he gave, the more it came back tenfold (as long as he didn't give with the *expectation* of receiving). By becoming a giver, you will be living in a space of abundance and gratitude. In doing so, you will find that you will attract far more success into your life. And you will feel that the money that you are earning has far more meaning and impact. This also fends off the guilty feeling that can sometimes creep in when people start becoming wealthy. You might start questioning whether you deserve to live so much better than the rest of the world. By using some of your money to do good for others, you will instead feel driven and fulfilled.

So now we are at 20 percent off the top, leaving 80 percent to live on. I know what some may be thinking right about now. You're screaming out loud, "I can't even pay my bills with 100 percent of my current income, and you're telling me to take away 20 percent and make it happen with only the remaining 80 percent?" Let me ask you this. If bill collectors are already calling you already based on 100 percent of your income not being enough to pay bills, won't they call you the same based on 80 percent? I doubt they will be any louder or ruder to you. The biggest question that I have for you is, "Who is more important to you — you and your family *or* the people to whom you owe your debts?" You better have answered the former and not the latter! I am not advocating not paying your debts, because you will — in full — in due time. But you have to put your head on your pillow at night knowing that for once, you are finally building your wealth (even when you are starting from under water). Day by day as your Wealth Account grows, your confidence grows with it. You will become more productive, and you will find yourself earning more. That 80 percent will grow, and your bills will get paid. And as your journey unfolds, at some point the debt will vanish and you will be *debt free* ... with a massive, growing net worth.

So be disciplined about that 20 percent off the top. *Paying yourself first at least 10 percent of every dollar you earn is not an option.* Let me stop and say this as boldly as I can: If you will not do this, you will *never* get wealthy.

Debt Free is the New Lamborghini

Do you want to wield the ultimate status symbol? Get debt free. Seriously. Being debt free is the most desirable financial achievement in the world today. Entire nations are imploding under the weight of their financial distress. Once successful companies are shuttering their doors forever. (Remember Blockbuster Video? Montgomery Ward's? Compaq?) Personal bankruptcies are at an all-time high. American consumers alone owe a staggering $11.86 *trillion* in debt (as of this writing), and our students are carrying a crippling $1.21 trillion in student loans. The burden of all of this debt is not only financially devastating but psychologically paralyzing as well.

Wouldn't it feel amazing to be debt free? I bet you would feel liberated to owe nobody. The weight of debt on people's shoulders is one of the main causes of stress, and a leading cause of marital arguments. When people say money is not important, I don't get that. If it's not important, why does it cause so much strife? One of my goals for building a network marketing business is to help people get on the other side of money. I don't want to teach people just how to make money, but rather how never to be a slave to it again. I want people to rid themselves of the stress that comes from debt, and to live happier, more fulfilled lives.

For many, the dream of being debt free is just that — a dream. Of course everyone would love the joy of not owing anything to anyone. But why do so few ever get completely out of debt? The reason is most people have no *plan*. You *have* to have a plan to get there. What has your plan been thus far? Was it just hoping that the debt would just disappear over time? I find that the people who don't have a plan to get out of debt usually find their debt doing nothing but *grow.*

Let's remember, part of your plan is to pay yourself first and build your Wealth Account. Alongside this investing/saving strategy, you also must be constantly reducing your debt to others. This part requires us to use some common sense. What debt should you pay off first? Start out by taking all of your bills and lining them up across your kitchen table. Arrange them in the order of highest interest rate to lowest. The rule of thumb that often makes the most sense is to pay off the highest rate debt first, as it is costing you the most money to carry. This is usually your credit card debt. Then you might have student loans, and then at the bottom is likely the mortgage on your home. (You should check your mortgage interest rate against the prevailing mortgage rates today in the market. If your rate is 1 ½ percent higher than the market, it may make sense to refinance this debt to lower your rate and payment.)

When you borrow money to pay for something, you must consider how much the interest charges will be to determine the actual price you will end up paying for that purchase. For example, if you buy a car for $30,000 with an interest rate of 5 percent over a five-year loan, add $3.968 interest to the principle purchase price. So you really end up paying $33,968, not $30,000. If you buy a computer for $800 on your credit card, and assuming you are not paying the full credit balance off each month, you are really paying much more for that computer. Let's assume your card's interest rate is 15 percent, and that you finally pay the computer off in three years. Add $198.36 in interest charges to the initial price tag, for an actual cost of $998.36! This is why I don't believe in buying on credit cards unless you pay it off in full at the end of the month to avoid these interest charges.

Is all debt created equal? There may be good debt and bad debt. Let me attack credit cards first. For me, I use credit cards for payment convenience, and my bank account automatically pays it off each month. Therefore, I never pay interest on this money. And I get reward points on those purchases. But for most people, credit card debt is bad.

You spent money that you did not have, assuming you are not paying off the balance every month. Spending money that you don't have on purchases that are not intended to make you money is sending you in the opposite direction of growing wealth or becoming debt free. We will cover this topic shortly when we discuss creating a personal budget. Credit card debt is usually the most expensive, often running 15 percent or more in interest rates. Your goal may always have been to pay the minimum payment each month, but this is what the bank *wants* you to do. Understand one thing — the banks *do not* want you to ever pay off your credit card balance. When you do, they stop earning money from you! They want you to keep rolling your balance forward every month, just making your minimum payment to keep you in good standing.

My goal for you is to pay down this balance with everything you can, as fast as you can. I use credit cards because they are a convenient (and safer than debit cards) way to pay for things. But I pay my balance off in full every month. So I urge you to use credit cards only if you will do the same. Otherwise, the interest charges erode the wealth you are attempting to accumulate.

So this begs the question: "Should I still pay myself 10 percent off the top and put it into my Wealth Account and then deal with the credit card debt from the remaining income?" This is an important question. This is where we have to understand numbers. Let's estimate that your invested money will yield between a 5-10 percent return. But your credit card debt is at 15 percent. You will be losing more money by investing because of the negative delta (difference). So for this reason, I would absolutely suggest that you first wipe out your credit card debt. Once this debt is cleared, then you can begin building your Wealth Account. Either way, you are affecting your net worth. While carrying credit card debt, your net worth may be in the negative. Bringing that number back to zero is improving your net worth. Then as your net worth goes positive, watch how your stress fades and your confidence grows. Life will take on a new zest.

Good Debt vs. Bad Debt

Is there really such a thing as "good debt?" Let's peg the average return on your investments at 10 percent. Any debt that costs you less than 10 percent is not really bad debt as you crunch the numbers. This is true as long as your money is being directed into investments that truly earn you more than what you are paying to service debt. So the first goal is to pay off all debts that are higher than your investment returns.

For most people, the ultimate goal is to get flat out debt free altogether. In simplest terms, that should be your goal, too. But at some point you might become a more savvy investor. You may calculate that you can increase your wealth by carrying some debt. For example, if your mortgage rate is only 4 percent, and you can get 10 percent return by investing, it makes sense to carry a mortgage because your net affect is 6 percent positive. On top of that, the government in some countries like the U.S. allows you to write off the interest on your mortgage. (As of 2014, that maximum mortgage amount is $1.1 million.) So in essence, the government is paying for part of your house payment. As much as I like the idea of being debt free, I also like making money. So I personally carry the maximum mortgage on my home, thus giving me money borrowed at 4 percent so that I can get a much higher return on my own cash and pocket the difference.

For those of you in the early stages of teaching yourselves about money, I suggest keeping it simple and making it your priority to go *Debt Free ASAP*. That ought to be your mantra. Some will put the words on their dream boards. Some will write the words on their bathroom mirrors. I am not totally opposed to this. But remember that we get more of what we focus on. So even though we are saying we want to get rid of debt, we are still *talking* about debt. If you are motivated by a war or attack on something bad, then that's fine. But I would rather you keep your focus on the positive, and write on your mirror or dream board — BUILD WEALTH or BUILD NET WORTH. The reason is that being debt free merely brings you to ground zero. You are not wealthy just because you are out of debt. You are out of the negative. The danger is in setting our goals too low. If you set a goal and hit that goal but are still not happy, then you set the goal too low in the first place. Your expectations of what life would be like after achieving that goal will let you down.

Proclaim Your Goals

I am glad we are on the topic of goals. There's an old saying that *if you don't know where you want to go, any road will take you there.* Goals set us into motion chasing something each day with a sense of purpose. Goals help us overcome obstacles, fear, and adversity. The right goals will get you up in the morning, and keep you energized throughout the day. I simply cannot imagine living a life without goals, wandering aimlessly through the days.

The key to goals is that you must dig deep and find goals that motivate you — move you to act. Your goals can include others, but they essentially are yours.

I believe that goals must be:

- specific
- written
- attached to a deadline
- worthwhile
- shared with others.

MINDSET BONUS

Download FREE printable Wealth and Debt-Free Proclamations at *moneymindsetbook.com/free*

Many people have goals of how much income they desire to earn per month/year. But we need to go to the next level and have goals for that money you are earning. So give yourself a goal of creating wealth. Define it.

- How much money will you have invested?
- How much cash in the bank?
- How much will your investment income be per year?
- When will you achieve this?
- What will change in your life because this goal is met?

Along the way, just one of the steps to achieving your wealth goals will be to become debt free. Just remember, this is an important milestone, but not your end game! Debt free means you owe nothing to anybody ... but it could be possible that you don't have much wealth either. So focus on setting these goals, share them with your family so they understand the importance, and then go figure out how you will make it happen.

Let's stop right now and help you discover goals that ignite your fire, and let's write these goals down in the form of a proclamation.

I am officially **Debt Free** on this date:

_____

I feel liberated.

I have true freedom.

I am planning a celebration trip to:

_____

I will reward myself with:

_____

I am officially **wealthy** on this date:

_____

I have this much net worth on this date:

_____

I feel secure.

I have peace of mind.

My investments generate annual cash flow of:

_____

So you now have put your mind to work on creating *specific* goals that move you. You have *written* them down. You attached *deadlines* to them. You decided these are *worthwhile* goals. And you can now *share* them with people in your life. An essential part of turning goals into reality is speaking them into your mindset every day. Reinforcing positive thoughts will burn the belief into your soul that you are accomplishing your goals. So here is a possible Daily Affirmation you can read aloud to yourself every morning and every night:

DAILY WEALTH AFFIRMATION

I am focused every day on building my wealth. I love money in all the good I will use it for. My financial freedom allows me to call my own shots, live life on my own terms, and I am excited about today. I am enjoying the wealth-building journey, because I know that what I learn and grow through will be just as valuable as the empire I am building. I am smart with my money and I am a great financial role model. I do not spend money frivolously. Every dollar I save I can invest. Every dollar I invest increases my empire. As my empire grows, so does my ability to influence others and to be a resource to support great causes and help others. I have the Wealth Mindset, and I am attracting wealth every day, including today.

Put this affirmation in front of you for easy access every day. Go onto our website to print a gorgeous copy for yourself.

Buy-In

It is critically important that you contemplate how these goals

MINDSET BONUS

Download FREE printable Wealth and Debt-Free Proclamations at *moneymindsetbook.com/free*

and your new mindset will impact those around you. If you are married or have children, this might instigate a change in lifestyle. Where you used to spend freely, take them places and buy them things … suddenly you have become this money monster. You have cut off the money tree and they aren't going to like it one bit. This is why you must get their buy-in on this new vision and game plan. They must see *why* you want to make these changes, and most importantly show them what's in it for them. If they do not feel the same way about your mission to cut spending and use excess revenues to invest in the future, you will have one unhappy situation.

Your value system may be changing. But theirs is still the same as it was yesterday. So you will need to work on convincing them to get on the same page as you. How? You will sell them on the *vision* of your future dream lifestyle, one enveloped in wealth, security, and freedom. In essence, you are going to

have to recruit them onto your team. It will take everyone operating as a team — *for* the team. They will need to find their
own ways to cut spending habits. They will need to support
the frugality going forward, rather than undermine your ef-
forts. If they have bought into the grand vision of becoming
debt free, financially independent, and wealthy, you will move
more easily towards your goals.

Another way to get your family on the same page with you is
to read this book together. Study it and use it to help create
your plan. Some family members might have a W-2 mindset
and might not have the same entrepreneurial blood running
through their veins. Inch them toward your world by watching entrepreneurial shows on TV, reading the right books, and
even sharing stories of people who have made it. Help them to
envision what they picture as their dream lifestyle, and then
show them stories of how people have achieved that through
the same business model as yours, and by developing a wealth-
builder mindset. Help them to see themselves as *unbroke*.

Using jars as a living metaphor can make it real. There are fun
ways — especially with children — to get their buy in. For
example, many parents I've mentored in network marketing
have used the children's desire to take a trip to Disney World.
So they had their kids cut out pictures of Mickey Mouse, the
Princess, or their favorite characters. They got a huge plas-
tic jar and glued the pictures to the side. They told the kids

that every time mom or dad goes to a business meeting, they would each get 50 cents to put into the jar. Once the jar is filled up, they would use this money to take the family to Disney World. You wouldn't believe how excited the kids got. They would ask, "Mom, why aren't you going to a meeting tonight?" How's that for a reversal? That's true buy-in. What if you did that for the wealth-building plan buy-in as well? Find ways for the household to contribute to the wealth jar, and once it fills up and goes into the bank, the family gets to go do something amazing.

How to Keep the Money You Make

It's not how much you make, it's how much you *keep* that matters most. Being a 1099 independent business owner, you get tax advantages that people who are employees do not get. The typical home-based business owner can legitimately save anywhere from $2,000-$5,000 a year (or much more) of in-pocket tax savings just by operating a small business in pursuit of making a profit — even if they don't actually turn a profit! Just signing up for a network marketing business is not enough. You must be pursuing profits by doing money-making activities. Be prudent about documenting your activities so if you are ever questioned, you can emphatically demonstrate that you had the intent to make a profit. As long as you can prove this, you will have the ability to write off many expenditures as business expenses. In other words, you deduct those expenses from your income total *before* paying taxes on the lowered amount.

Do you need to have income that is greater than your expenses to be able to write them off? Actually, no you don't. To the extent that you spent more than you earned, the excess expense can be carried over and applied against your income in future years. This is called a business loss carry-forward. Your business loss can even be deducted from the ordinary income from your job. This is often the case, as new network marketers may spend more than they earn from the new business in the beginning. This does not mean your business is not working. It just means businesses take time to build and become profitable, and the government understands this. So if you lost/spent more than you earned for the first couple of years in your network marketing business (which is common in any business start up), it comes back to you in a way. You will carry that loss forward and deduct it in the first profitable year. So keep investing and planting seeds to build your business.

Just so you can appreciate the tax benefits of building a business like this, let's briefly touch on the difference between you and a person who gets paid as a W-2 employee. As an employee you get a salary, the government subtracts their taxes from the full amount, and then you get what's left over. But as a 1099 business owner, you earn your commissions, you deduct your business expenses, then pay taxes based *on that lower amount.*

Here is a rudimentary example:

Job Salary — $50,000
Taxable Income — $50,000
Government taxes at 20 percent — $10,000 taxes paid

Network Marketing Income — $50,000
Subtract Writeoffs/Deductions — Minus $10,000
Taxable Income — $40,000
Taxes at 20 percent — $8,000 taxes paid

The great thing about running a business out of your home is you get to write off any expenses that are connected to your pursuit of a profit. Here are some examples (get specific details from a tax expert/CPA):

Home office expense — If 20 percent of the square footage of your home is used for business (office, supplies storage, etc), you get to write off that percentage of your mortgage/rent payment, of the utilities, and of house cleaning

Car expense — You can choose to write off actual costs for your car, gas, maintenance, washes, *or* you can write off a certain amount per mile you drove the car for business purposes. In 2014, the rate is 56 cents per business-driven mile! (Be sure to keep a daily log of the business miles). So if you drove 20 miles to drive to a business appointment, you write off $11.20. The government, in essence, just paid for a few gallons of your gas!

Meals/Entertainment — Any time you meet with prospects for a bite or conduct a team meeting at a restaurant, you get to write off a percentage of your check.

Travel/Hotels — Any travel that is business related (meaning you did business as the reason for the trip), you can write off your plane ticket and lodging. You are allowed to take in the scenery and enjoy yourself too.

Here are other categories that may be eligible to be written off.

Tools/Supplies/Printing
Website design/hosting
Telecommunications
Event tickets for briefings, trainings, conventions
Awards/Contest prizes
Contributions to Retirement Plans
Office Furniture

You can even hire your spouse or kids, which will entitle you to tax advantages as well. For example, if you hire your spouse, this will allow you to write off your medical expenses! Otherwise, this is not normally a tax write-off.

Be sure to keep *all* receipts and records. Even if it is a toll in your car for $3, every dollar adds up. Track *everything*. There are many ways to do this. Some people are old fashioned, throwing every paper receipt in a file box and sorting it out at the end of the year. Others are more modern and use tax software and do expense entries each night to stay totally on top of it.

One tip I use is to always use one business credit card or checking account for all business use. This way everything is always tracked by simply pulling my account statement. Of course you will have your box of paper receipts to journal every expense should you ever get an audit letter. There are now apps that allow you to do that on your mobile device by simply snapping a photo of the receipt.

In addition to tracking your expenditures, keep a physical calendar of your activities. This might be needed to prove that you are actually pursing the business in the early days when your profits are lower than your expenses. Keep a log of the training calls you are listening to, events you are attending, appointments you are conducting, and prospecting activities you are doing. Order updated company material, tools and product on a regular basis. Basically, do what you would expect to do to build your business. Just track and document it.

Paying Your Taxes

Please note that this section is written from my perspective as an American, Readers in other countries would do well to heed the tax laws of their respective governments.

We talked about the benefits of home business tax deductions. Tax codes and rules change often, so be sure to consult with an expert tax accountant. The next key to wealth building is to treat taxes seriously. Pay what you owe, and *pay on time*.

Our taxes pay for the police, fire department, schools, roads, military, and the freedoms we all enjoy. As often as I think that our tax rates are far too high, I pay them with pride. I once had a goal to earn six figures in a year. Then I had a goal to pay six figures in taxes in a year. Now I pay multiple six figures in taxes. I feel lucky to have been blessed enough to earn this money, so I pay my share to help keep the system going for us all. I see many people try to cheat the system and not pay taxes. Let me warn you, it will *always* catch up with you. Most of the time, the government will track you down ... and if they don't, karma will! Just live by the rule of doing what's right when no one is looking. That's what it means to have character.

MINDSET BONUS

Download a FREE

Monthly

Personal Budget at

moneymindsetbook.com/free

Paying *on time* is critical. First of all, if you are late in paying, you tack on fines and penalties. This costs you even more than your fair share, and wastes money that you could have invested. This is often caused by not being diligent as the money comes in, and not carving off your estimated taxes as you go along. If you estimate that you will be in a 20 percent tax bracket, then put aside 20 percent of every check you get for taxes. Put this into a separate account from your spending account. Do not touch this money under any circumstances!

Once you get through your first year and have established a record of earnings, you will be expected to pay "quarterly estimated taxes" from then on. In other words, you will need to estimate what your earnings will be for the calendar year, deduct your estimated expenses, multiply the net amount by your tax rate, and pay one fourth of that every quarter. If at year-end you did not earn quite that much and you overpaid, or you underestimated your business expenses, you will request a refund when you file your tax return that spring.

I have witnessed many network marketers fall short on paying taxes. They let it get away from them, and next thing they know they owe the government many thousands of dollars more than they possess. The last person you want to owe money to is the government. They can garnish your income and even seize your assets. Be smart; be disciplined. As I have said before, "You must have self discipline, or the world will discipline you. Either way, you will get disciplined."

Set a Personal Budget

You have to inspect what you expect. Budgeting is planning your cash flow. How much will you have coming in, and how much will be going out? If you don't track it, you cannot control it. This is the common problem with most people who struggle financially. If I ask them to show me their budget, they look back at me with a confused look on their face. Budgeting was never taught in high school, and not taught in general college studies. Most parents don't have a budget, so they surely have not taught this to their kids. The good news is that if you decide to act on the principles of this book and create a budget, you will be far ahead of the crowd.

Readers of this book can download a free sample personal budget. (See Mindset Bonus.) Once downloaded, you will see that you are expected to set a goal for spending in each category, then, at month-end, write in your actual amount spent. This will give you the ability to review where you are overspending, and help you to establish your goals for next month to improve. By seeing your spending habits on paper, it will allow you to get a good visual on your financial picture. You will be able to see what expenses truly are necessary and cannot be reduced, and which ones might have some play. Of course you always want to try to raise your top line income number. But to build wealth faster, look for ways to cut down on personal spending at the same time.

MINDSET BONUS

Download a FREE Monthly Business Budget at moneymindsetbook.com/free

Set a Business Budget

Just like your life needs a personal budget to plan and track your income and your living expenses, so does your business. Your business will require some investment to start, and to build. There are costs for lead generation, websites, materials, cell phones, transportation, etc. Some might think the more you spend, the more you will make. This is not always true, but generally it has some merit. The key to your business budget is to be thoughtful in your planning and review. I initially set a goal of spending $300 in a month to generate some prospects. If I found that after the campaign it returned $500 to me, I would scale it up the next month to double the spend. If that $600 yielded a proportionate return, I could make a decision to continue moving the campaign forward. But if I budgeted monies towards a project and it did not bear fruit, I would review the plan and make changes accordingly.

Money does not come from thin air. Nobody has an unlimited budget for spending. Knowing this, it is imperative that you decide how much total money you have to invest each month into your business. (Feel free to download the Mindset Bonus sample that I have used for my own business budget). Then you can allocate portions of that total to the various activities or needs of your business. Remember, you have to see your cash flow in order to make the best decisions. Therefore, getting your budget on paper is very important.

THE INVESTING MINDSET

How to Invest Your Money

So you've earned some money. You have deducted your expenses and paid taxes on the taxable portion. Now what's the next step towards growing this net income and becoming wealthy? It's no small step that you've gotten here! Whether you have a surplus of $50 a month to invest, or $500, or $5,000, the plan will be much the same. There are many ways to invest your money and put it to work for you. As I have also heard it, "Send your money out into the world and have it come back with friends!"

What I have found is you can rank the investment ideas in order of return and importance. You also must ask whether you want to invest your money to grow your current business, or to be invested into something completely separate. Here are my investment areas:

1. Back into your business
2. Into yourself
3. Stocks
4. Bonds
5. Money Market / CDs
6. Real estate
7. Life Insurance
8. Other Businesses
9. Tax Deferred plans

Let's explore each of these investment options.

Investing Back into Your Business

I had a mentor who once told me that the best investment I could make, better than any stock pick, would be to invest back into my network marketing business. This business is your/my cash machine. If you can pump money back into the machine to make it turn out even bigger profits, what could be better? So this is what I did. I looked for every way that I could employ my money to grow my machine. Here are some things I invested money into:

- Tools — videos, DVDs, brochures, websites
- Buying business opportunity leads to recruit from
- Hosting luncheons and dinners
- Running team contests and incentives
- Personal development for my team

For example, I learned that whoever moves the most tools into the marketplace will make the most money. I have lived by this and taught this for the last 16 years. The more tools my team and I got into prospects' hands each month, the higher our recruiting numbers climbed. In other words, the more we spent on tools, the more we made in profits.

If I spent $100 to buy 100 DVDs, look at what happened.
- 100 prospects get a DVD
- 20 actually watch it
- 10 have interest
- 5 become customers
- 3 become distributors

At the lower level in my company's comp plan, that makes me over $500 right off the bat. But I also now have three new recruits to work with and exponentially grow my team and my override income. This could mean thousands of dollars per year or even per month in new overrides. What stock could I buy for $100 that would predictably give me this kind of return? What real estate?

I spent time teaching this logic to my team, and in doing so, they duplicated the investment/spending. Their recruiting increased, which further grew my business. So, in effect, I have found that investing back into the business is the absolute best, most predictable payoff.

Investing into Yourself

It can be argued that investing into yourself should top the list, even above investing into your business. But I will rank this at number two, only because it is not as immediate or as easy to measure. As I stated earlier, in order for your income to grow, *you* need to grow. If you ever want to earn six figures, or even seven figures a year, you need to become the person who deserves such an income. You must grow your mind, your attitude, your skills, and your personality.

Here are some ways that I have invested into myself over the years:

- Books
- Tapes/audios
- Attending seminars
- Training events
- All of the above for people on my team

In the grand scheme of things, this area does not require an awfully large amount of financial investment. It is mostly time investment, in reading books and listening to audios. Once in a while you might spend $500 to attend a workshop in a certain skill you want to develop. This cost might turn into $1,500 when you factor in a plane ticket, hotel room, and meals. Your company likely has a monthly event to attend for learning, recognition and motivation. This might cost a whopping $20 for a ticket. I have found this $20 investment to be one of the biggest returns for me over my career. It pains me to hear people say they cannot afford to attend such events, or to simply decide it is not worth their time. These people are sadly mistaken, and are, frankly, uncoachable. And for this reason, I predict they will fail.

Author and speaker Charlie "Tremendous" Jones always taught, "You will be the same person five years from now that you are today, except for the people you meet and the books you read." We need to get around people who could have a positive influence on us. These monthly events and workshops allow us to get into an environment that promotes growth and success. And this gets us around people who can help us succeed. We must stop hanging around with people who have our same problems, and get around those who have our solutions.

When I learned of a great book or audio, I would buy hundreds of them to get into my team's hands. A *follower* will read a book and say, "That was a great book," and then put it aside. A *leader* says, "This is a good book, I need to get my entire team reading it!" That leader promotes it day and night, and uses it as a tool to train and develop his/her people. So invest in the development of yourself and your people.

Investing in Stocks

One great thing about investing in the stock market is that the market provides liquidity. It is very simple to buy stocks these days online in just a few seconds. And it is just as easy to go online and sell stock, should you want to liquidate or sell it to raise some cash.

What you should do first is decide what kind of investor you want to be — passive or active. Do you want to invest in a fund and let the professional fund managers pick the stocks and manage your account for you, or do you want to take on the job of picking, buying, and managing this yourself? If you are brand new to investing, I suggest you go with a fund. This way, your money can be invested and can grow, without you losing your focus and having to become a stock and financial planning expert.

There are mutual funds and index funds. A mutual fund is simply a grouping of stocks picked by the fund manager. A typical mutual fund may have one hundred stocks in it. This gives you diversification across many companies, which reduces your risk of a few companies doing poorly and losing much of your investment. These funds can be found grouped in many ways. You can buy a fund focused on companies in technology, energy, transportation, real estate, industrials, or others. This gives you exposure to a number of stocks in a single investment vehicle. The premise of investing in a particular mutual fund is that the fund manager you select might be a better stock picker than other managers, and thus outperform the rest in the market. So investors will often research mutual fund managers' track records over the last several years to find the managers who are in their groove and investing in the right places.

Mutual funds should be bought with some understanding of how they function. You are giving your money to the manager to buy the stocks he has chosen for the fund. During the time you own this fund, you will likely see the manager sell some of the stocks and replace them with others that he feels are better investments at that time. You will pay fees to the fund managers for their expertise, for their service, for conducting transactions. At the time of this writing, the average mutual fund fees are about 1.44 percent of the value of your investment each year. While this is not a high percentage, you need to ask and know what the precise fees are that you will be charged. Even fractional percentages can chip away at your long-term wealth accumulation. A half percent, compounded over years, could mean the difference of hundreds of thousands of dollars!

Index funds are a bit different. An index fund is said to provide broad market exposure, low operating expenses, and low portfolio turnover. Instead of hiring fund managers to actively select which stocks or bonds the fund will hold, an index fund buys all (or a representative sample) of the companies in a specific index, like the S&P 500 Index or the Dow Jones Industrial index. The goal of an index fund is to track the performance of a specific market benchmark as closely as possible. That's why you may hear it referred to as a "passively managed" fund. If the broader market goes up, your investment goes up with it. You are not betting on a small, select list of companies. You are invested in the whole market.

- Some index funds give you exposure to potentially thousands of securities in a single fund, so you have *lower risk because of broader diversification.*

- Because index funds hold investments until the index itself changes (which is less frequent), they generally have *lower management and transaction costs.* Owning an index fund can cost as little as .25 percent in fees (much different from the 1.44 percent in actively managed mutual funds). That's almost six times less!

- Broad index funds generally don't trade companies inside the fund as much as actively managed funds might, so they typically generate less taxable income. This tax efficiency reduces the drag on your investment performance.

Index funds are likely your best choice, not mutual fund where money managers are chasing performance. Many top experts like Warren Buffett, the wealthiest man on Earth (at over $64 billion), have warned that you are very unlikely to beat the S&P index. Buffett says there's less than 10 percent chance! So with slim chances of getting a higher return *and* with mutual fund managers taking higher fees, an index fund is the obvious way to go.

Picking Stocks Yourself

OK, so what if you really want to pick your own stocks? Nowadays, anyone can set up an online trading account with a reputable stock trading company. You can fund it with as little as a few hundred dollars. You could even buy one share of a $20 stock if you want. Of course this is not recommended, because even with a low $7 transaction fee you really paid $27 for that share. So you are at a loss unless the stock price appreciates to a price higher than $27, and if it costs you $7 more to execute the sale transaction, you need the price to be higher than $34 to just break even. Therefore, when it comes to investing in stocks, it makes sense to do so when you have a sizable amount to invest. I would say that investing at least several hundred dollars or more at a time is the minimum, for the reason I just shared. If you do not yet have a few thousand dollars in cash ready to invest into stocks, make it your plan to start building your cash pile. "Cash is King" is a famous line in the investment world. When you have cash on the sidelines not yet invested, you can be poised and ready to strike when a great investment idea or stock idea comes along, or if the market comes way down and creates a very attractive entry point.

Let's assume you have a few thousand in cash, and you are ready to deploy it into the stock market — which is my favorite investment vehicle. I would recommend doing your research and finding a financial advisor/stock broker who has a great reputation and strong track record for his clients. It can be dangerous trying to be a stock picker yourself if you do not have experience in this world. In addition, it takes considerable time to study the companies you are interested in buying into, and to keep up with them on an ongoing basis once you own their stock.

Frankly, I have struggled with this distraction in my own life. I found myself watching the stock market throughout the day, which was taking my eye off the cash machine that makes me the money to invest with in the first place (my network marketing business)! So promise me that you won't make that same mistake and wake up one day and suddenly become a day trader. Don't let the stock market take hold of your brain. It's very easy to allow this to happen. You want your investments to be mostly passive. This does not mean you throw your money into something and blindly let it ride. Of course you need to maintain knowledge of your investments going forward. This is why many successful people have a paid professional to help them make these investments and watch over them daily *for* them.

If you happen to want to invest in a few specific companies and you feel up to the challenge of learning, just be very careful. But for the sake of this example, let me give you at least a starter's overview of how this works.

When you buy a stock, you own a piece of that company and its earnings. You might be investing to speculate that the stock price will appreciate or go up in price. In other words you buy a share for $30 hoping it goes up to $50 so you can sell for the $20 profit. Or you might be buying a stock because it pays a quarterly cash dividend, and you are buying that cash flow. Many companies that are generating free cash flow (profits) choose to distribute/pay out a portion of their profits to their shareholders. This dividend is measured as a percentage of its share price called its *yield*. So if you buy a stock at $100 a share, and the dividend per share is $5 per year, the "cost" yield to you on your money invested is 5 percent (because your cost basis was $100). If the stock price goes up to $200 and the dividend remains at $5, your cost yield is still 5 percent, but your "current" yield is 2.5 percent (because the current value you could sell the stock for is now $200).

Are dividends important? It depends on why you are investing. If you only care about the value of the stock prices going up, then not so much. But if you are investing for cash flow, meaning you want your portfolio of stocks to be sending you cash dividends throughout the year to live on, then yield is important. I have invested in some stocks that did well in both price appreciation and dividend yield. But of course, you win some and you lose some when picking stocks as a speculator. It is riskier to chase appreciation, though I have done very well myself in this area. But I have a higher risk tolerance because I can afford to take a hit. If you don't have the guts for that risk and if losing some of your investment would alter your immediate life, you might place more emphasis on yields and stick with stocks with proven track records of paying cash dividends.

"Pigs get fed, but hogs get slaughtered." I heard this quote many times on CNBC television, but it did not sink in until years later. What this means is that greed is good, but you should not get *too* greedy. If you bought a stock at $30 and it jumps to $60 in a relatively short period, you may be tempted to get really greedy and try to ride it to $70 or $80 or $100. But hold up … you just *doubled* your money! Do you really want to risk your profits and possibly give some of the gains back?

Let me share with you my personal story to demonstrate this. I bought shares of Apple stock in 2011 for around $350 a share. And I went in heavy with over $1 million invested, and even bought some via call options (a leveraged way to buy the rights to buy shares in the future at a certain price point). One year later, the shares were trading at over $700 a share and my position (shares and options) was worth almost $4 million! But I got too greedy, and decide to hold on and see if the shares might go up to $800 before I would unload them. Well, the price peaked at $711 and then began a decline that I thought would be short lived. The stock kept going down as I held on and it stopped its decent at $380 a share in 2013. So almost all of my gains were wiped out. I should have taken some of my money off the table as it was climbing into the $600s, and I would have protected my gains and had that wealth.

Luckily for me, I had to ability to stay on for the ride and I had enormous confidence in Apple and felt the market would soon see how they were misjudging Apple. I am very fortunate that I was right. Here it is, two years later, and the stock is trading today at $920 a share (shares split 7-for-1, so this adjusted to a trading price of $129). So I ended up making a few million on the position.

But some of the time the story doesn't turn out that well.

I bought $100,000 worth of shares in Avon at $28 when it came down from $42. I felt this stock would go back up to $42 in a few months. Well, it did go in that direction to about $32, which is a respectable 15 percent gain, in just a few weeks. But I held on for more. Some news came out that the company was having some challenges overseas and the stock went down even more. I ended up selling this position at $16 a share, for a 50 percent loss of $50,000. And thankfully I sold when I did, because those shares are trading today at just over $7.

Here is another story of "success," but one in which I was my own worst enemy. I went to high school with the founder of

Under Armour. So when Kevin Plank started his company, I had an interest in watching his business grow. When the company went public in 2006 at (split-adjusted price) $6 per share, I soon began buying some shares. Within the first year, my money doubled. But I always saw Under Armour as a long-term play. I just had the solid belief that this company was going to keep growing and growing and one day become a formidable competitor of Nike.

In 2009 just after the stock market crashed, I was able to buy Under Armour shares at $3.60! So I bought 2,000 shares at this price. But I started getting caught up in the trading game. Because the market can go up and down, I thought when it hit $7 I would sell those 2,000 shares for a nice profit, wait for the shares to come back down and buy them back, pocketing the difference. Well, the price never came back down. In fact it doubled in six months, and doubled again in six more months. I got this feeling that I better buy more before it keeps running, so I did. I put $200,000 into UA shares at $16, and sold them at $22, expecting the market to pull back and give me a chance to buy them back lower.

The market did no such thing.

So I ended up buying more shares at $28, and I played that game again selling them at $38. The price never came back down to let me buy back in at a lower price. I played this game two more times, and each time pocketed some profits but had to pay up for more shares. This last year, I finally learned my lesson and put $1 million in at $65 and swore to myself that I am no longer going to trade in and out, but rather will hold the shares for the next 10 years like Warren Buffett does and advises. I am happy to report that those shares are trading to-day at $85 a share! But if I had only held all of those shares along the way and kept adding to my position to align with my conviction in the strength of Under Armour's business, my position would be worth several million dollars.

Here is the moral of this last story: You *must* choose a strategy. You can either be a day trader who spends half of your day watching your portfolio and trying to time the market, buying and selling often, *or* you can choose to follow in the footsteps of Warren Buffett, the richest investor in the world. Buffett only buys stock in companies that he believes in for the long haul, and holds that stock for at least 10 years. I have person-ally made more money in the stocks I invested in for the long term than I did making short-term plays. But more impor-tantly, I must point out that watching the stocks daily took too much of my focus and time away from my network marketing business. So who knows how to calculate what that cost me?

One strategy that I feel has merit is using the "20 percent sell rule" as a way of preserving big stock gains. As you watch your stock climb, you get that excited feeling as you see your wealth increasing. It's almost like butterflies in your stomach. You are picturing that new home or boat you've been dreaming of buying coming to fruition sooner than you expected! But this dream can evaporate just as fast if something happens with the company or if the market turns sour. Those butterflies fly away and now you have a pit in your stomach and you feel like throwing up because you watched the gains disappear or even turn into a loss.

This is why many prudent investors have a rule where they start taking some of their profits off the table once a stock increases by over 20 percent from their purchase price. This way they lock in some gains, and let the rest of the money ride in case the stock continues to climb. If the rise continues, you can take some more off the table, and soon you might have your initial investment back. Now you are playing with the house's money! And you are free to invest that principle into a new stock or investment. This is in the same rationale as "pigs get fed, and hogs get slaughtered." You never go broke taking profits. Always remember that.

As you can tell, I believe strongly in investing in the stock market. As you begin investing in stocks, I encourage you to do so with a long-term mentality. Don't buy stock today with the hope of selling it after Christmas for a profit. Buy companies that you believe in and have strong growth out in front of them. Let your investments be more passive so you can keep your focus cranking your primary income source. Try to avoid riskier plays until you have plenty of net worth, and you can afford to take risks and absorb some investments that go bad. I have always heard the advice, "Never invest money that you cannot afford to lose." This is sage advice. You are only investing from the Wealth Account that you have set aside for this very purpose, and it is not money that is required for your living expenses.

Again, I would remind you if you are a brand new investor, to start by getting into an Index Fund. There are some funds like Vanguard that mirror the S&P 500 index.

Investing in Bonds

Bonds are a bit different from stocks. Bonds are bought more for yield, not really for appreciation. If you buy a municipal bond that pays 8 percent, you are merely trying to limit risk and receive an interest payment on the loan you are making to that entity. Bonds have four yields: coupon (the bond interest rate fixed at issuance), current (the bond interest rate as a percentage of the current price of the bond), and yield to maturity (an estimate of what an investor will receive if the bond is held to its maturity date). Non-taxable municipal bonds will have a tax-equivalent (TE) yield determined by the investor's tax bracket.

I know this sounds confusing, and frankly it's not that important right now for what we are covering today. I have never personally bought bonds myself, but my financial advisor has some included in my investment portfolio.

Investing in Money Market / CDs

The money market is investing in fixed-income securities. This is similar to the bond market, except that this investment is in short-term debt and money instruments. This means that they mature in less than a year, and are quite liquid.

Because these normally trade in very high denominations, retail investors like you and me cannot easily access them directly. But you can get in through money market mutual funds, or your bank may offer a money market bank account. Such accounts pool money from thousands of investors together to buy these securities. We had a "sweep account" like this for years, basically enabling the cash in my bank account to be swept into money market investments each night. Money market funds are considered low-risk investments, because they invest in well-established, solid corporations and in short-term government treasuries. Thus, these are considered to be a safe haven for your money. A big positive for these money market funds is that your gains are often tax exempt since they are investing in government securities. (Dividends are taxable, of course.)

Other ways to invest in the money market include T-bills (Treasury Bills) or CDs (certificates of deposit). The reason some people might wish to invest in this manner is to get a higher interest rate on their savings than a normal bank account will yield. And it is fairly liquid, meaning you can pull your cash out in shorter time frames. (CDs are a less liquid than money markets due to maturity dates.) The good thing is that these are relatively safe ways to keep your money and earn some interest income from it. I keep only a small portion in this type of vehicle, as I can get higher returns elsewhere like in stocks/equities (with a bit more risk attached). Talk with your banker about specifics.

Investing in Real Estate

I hear lots of people talk about getting into real estate investing. My background prior to going full time in network marketing was in real estate, both in selling and investing. I understand the allure. When you buy a house properly, you can potentially have positive monthly cash flow (difference of how much you collect in rent above your mortgage and carrying costs) *and* you can see the house value appreciate. I watched my father and what he did many years ago. He bought one house a year for quite a long time. His portfolio, over time, had those mortgages all paid off by the rents collected along the way. His tenants paid for the houses, which he now owns outright! His rental income every year is now stupendous. Of course, he still has to pay property taxes and maintain the houses, but he has great positive cash flow.

There are definite positives to buying houses. But what must you watch out for? Rents are subject to market conditions. Rents don't always stay the same. They can go up, but a glut of rentals on the market could cause the rents to go down. What would happen if you suddenly got less rental income each month than you have to pay in carrying costs? The house goes from a cash flow asset to a liability.

Repairs and maintenance must be expected. What would happen if the hot water heater broke, or the heating system in the winter went down? You will want to have enough liquid resources on hand to be able to stroke a check to pay thousands for such repairs. Exterior painting, new roof, new gutters, etc. — these can be expensive. I just had the air conditioner on one of my houses in Virginia go bad and it cost me $4,900 to replace. So you will need to be ready for these surprises at a moment's notice.

Vacancy is another concern. If you happen to have a time gap between tenants, would you be able to carry the costs for a few months with no rent monies coming in? On top of that, if you are like me, you might not want to spend the time (and money) to advertise the house for rent yourself. Hiring a real estate agent to list and secure a lease will typically cost you a full month's rent.

My point here is that you must factor these costs into your

investment equation if you are thinking of buying investment properties. My father had plenty of income from his main business coming in, and plenty of cash reserves, *before* he began accumulating the houses. I bought some houses along the way as well, just not one every year. I have watched my investment homes appreciate in value over the years, and in 2008 I saw them decline, too. Overall, the investments have yielded good returns on my capital. And my end game is to be like my father — own a real estate portfolio that is free and clear, throwing off passive cash flow forever.

But let me repeat: I did this *slowly* over time, and I had plenty of cash in the bank to do so. The idea of buying houses with no money down (because you have no money) is one of the most dangerous ideas I have ever seen. Believers beware. If you are buying with no money down while you have plenty of cash on hand, then you are finding great opportunities. More power to you!

Home Ownership — Rent vs. Own

Some of the best advice I got from my father, who was a major real estate company owner, was that it's better to own your home than rent. He always said, "When you rent a home, you are throwing that money down the drain and you will never see it again." The landlord who takes your rent is smiling because he/she is letting you pay their mortgage payments for them! You are buying them a house. At the end of the day (or the end of the mortgage term), they own a house that they can collect rents on forever! And they can sell this asset for cash should they choose. You, the renter, will eventually move out and take your belongings, leaving behind the home you paid for! You want to own the home you live in.

When you take out a mortgage loan to buy a house, you will be making payments that go toward the loan principle and also the interest on the loan amount. The money that goes to the principle is paying down the loan and building equity in the house. The interest is money that goes to the bank and does not build equity or your wealth. One good part about mortgage interest (what I call "good debt") is that the government in some countries (like the U.S.) allows you to write off your mortgage interest up to a loan amount limit of $1 million. The tax deduction is a very big benefit of home ownership. Basically, Uncle Sam is helping pay for you to own your home.

I have kept each home as I upgrade to a new home, and rent the previous one out. This has helped me build a small real estate investment portfolio. I want to follow in my father's footsteps of eventually having a string of houses that are all paid off, spitting out cash flow to me every month that I can live on. It's all about building assets. I started by buying my first home at age 24, for which I paid $175,000. That house now is worth $500,000. So in 20 years, the house tripled in value, *and* remember, I have collected rent for the last 13 years since

I moved out of it. That rent more than covers my mortgage payment, which means I have achieved the investor's goal of positive cash flow. I have bought other houses since. But it all started with me owning my own home first. Renters are simply on a path to nowhere if they want to build wealth.

How much house should you buy? What is your budget? The government learned its lesson during the meltdown of 2008 when sub-prime mortgages imploded and sent the U.S. into a deep recession. People were buying homes and getting mortgages they should never have qualified for. They often did not have substantiated income, and when the home values collapsed, the owners found themselves under water; they owed more to the bank than their home was worth. Foreclosures ripped through the nation. Billions and billions were lost. This would never have been allowed to happen if the government had been stricter on regulating the banks' loan qualifications for borrowers.

The best rule of thumb to guide you (don't worry, since the 2008 mortgage meltdown, banks won't let you overshoot now) is that your monthly house payment should be about one third of your gross monthly income. So if you make $6,000 a month, your house payment should be limited to $2,000. At a 5 percent interest rate, you are looking at a principle and interest payment of around $1,879 on a house price of $350,000. Add in taxes and insurance and you are pretty much right there. Remember, it's always a good idea to live below your means, even on the purchase of your home. You never want to be stretched to your limits, because one string of bad luck and you can lose your home.

Investing in Life Insurance

This is one investment I will write about but have chosen not to make myself. Please, insurance salespeople don't bother calling me. I am not interested! I do not believe that you have to invest in every conceivable strategy, and this one just isn't for me. There is no right or wrong. Life insurance is designed to be a death benefit to provide security for your family upon your death. For this purpose, it is smart to have this insurance. But when you have this marketed to you as an investment vehicle that can build cash value over time (and even let you borrow against it tax-free), it is not all that simple to say it's a no-brainer. Things might not go as you hope. The underlying investments might not perform as well as you were led to believe. You as the policyholder may not have the ongoing resources to fund the policy to the level you planned for. If you take out too much cash from your policy, it could trigger a tax event and you would have to come up with the money to pay these taxes. Lastly, should you decide to surrender to get out of the policy early, you will incur expensive penalties.

So, personally, I see value in buying a life insurance policy for the death benefit for your family more than as an investment vehicle.

Investing in Other Businesses

Once an entrepreneur has success in a business, it is easy to catch the fever and they want to have their hands in additional businesses on the side. I warn you that chasing two rabbits at the same time will ultimately result in catching neither. Especially trying to build multiple network marketing businesses. But if you really want to divert some of your time and attention to invest on the side in a traditional business, just be aware that the loss of laser focus can detract from your cash machine.

It is dangerous to be just an absent, passive investor in another person's business. It is very hard to have visibility, or to prevent the operator/owner or employees from stealing and/ or running the business improperly, especially if you are not hands-on. Therefore, I do not recommend it.

Here's a little story of what happened to me. My good friend's stepdad is the founder of a well-known casual dining franchise. My friend was a commercial real estate agent. I thought this was a no-lose combination to safely invest safely some of my network marketing income into opening some restaurants with him out of state. So I started writing the checks. We got the first location open. It seemed to be going OK, and I started writing bigger checks for the second location. By the time I asked to see the books to look over the accounting, I discovered that he was hiding so much from me. The restaurant was losing money every month. He was living off the money I was giving him for the second location. So I pulled the plug and lawyered up. When it was all said and done, I walked away with my bank account lighter by $760,000. That was an expensive lesson — in business and in friendship. I share this with you in hopes that you can learn from my experience and not go through an ordeal like this yourself.

If you choose to invest in another business, be sure you do your homework. Know the owner well, know the business well, be there constantly, make sure other successful investors are also involved with their money too. (You want multiple sets of eyeballs of people with skin in the game watching over it.) Keep in mind, investing in a business is not very liquid. If you ever need to pull out your cash quickly, don't count on it. You will have to find a willing and able buyer, which can take time — time you night not have.

Investing in Tax Deferred Plans

Any time the government lets you take some of your income and invest it *before* paying taxes on it first, do it! "Tax deferred" means you defer paying taxes until a later date. There are simple plans that let you do this, such as a 401K or a SEP (Simplified Employee Pension) IRA. The SEP IRA is a retirement plan designed to benefit small business owners and self-employed individuals. You are limited to a certain amount you can take from your income and contribute to the plan each year. In 2015, that limit was $53,000 and the amount is a percentage calculation of your net self-employment income or small business profits. (See a tax professional or research online for additional details). The more you can put away or invest tax-deferred dollars, the better. I always max out my limit every year! This is the best wealth-building decision I believe you can ever make.

Several years ago, one of my financial advisors encouraged me to set up a Defined Benefit Plan (DBP), which is a pension plan. One of my business mentors had been contributing to a DBP for years and he swore by the importance of setting mine up. For business owners earning in excess of $200,000 a year, it makes sense to consider this plan. These are more flexible than 401Ks and IRAs, and have much higher contribution limits. The way this works is you define/set the number for how much money you want your account (DBP) to be worth at a predetermined age. Say you want to have $2 million when you turn 65 years of age. Calculations will be made to determine how much you will be able to (have to commit to) contribute each year between now and age 65 to achieve this goal. This amount will vary each year depending on your account investment growth and your income. Your contributions should be managed by an investment advisor and put into safe investments. This is not where you will take risks and speculate, shooting for big returns, like you might do in a stock trading account.

The government is letting you defer tax on the front end while you are earning the money and likely in a higher income tax bracket, and then pay taxes upon distribution to you at the later age when you are likely in a lower tax bracket. Using an investment vehicle like a DBP allows you to be more diversified and protect your wealth, thus making you feel more secure.

Why Your Network Marketing Business is the Best Cash Machine

Wealthy people collect assets that throw off continuous cash flow. This is why network marketing is the ultimate business model. You get to establish countless points of distribution for selling your products by recruiting and creating a network of distributors. This override and residual income can be directed toward your wealth creation. It is a machine, and you must keep it turned on and printing money.

Let me put this into perspective, so that you understand the value of the business you have in your hands.

Option A - You have $1 million invested in bonds at a 5 percent return. This would generate an income of $50,000 a year.

Option B - Assuming you had the financial ability to buy one million dollars of real estate, you own ten $100,000 rental houses, and if each were throwing off $400 a month in net rental cash flow, you would have a gross income of $48,000. Of course, we have not considered the maintenance, toilets, furnaces, repairs, and vacancies, and other all-around headaches.

Option C - You build a network marketing business and recruit enough people to find ten builders, each generating $400 a month in override income to you. That's the same $50,000 a year, but without you having to be a landlord for 10 houses or having a million dollars cash to invest. Once you have established leadership in your team, you can step away and that business can continue to grow. But what you'll likely find is that you enjoy building this business so much, you will keep building more leaders and volume, and take your income to greater heights. You can scale this business as large as you want ... the sky is the limit because it requires no real capital investment!

Always remember that in network marketing, you are building a business of your own — an asset. I have watched one of my own upline mentors earn seven figures from the business, and then sell his business to a billionaire for seven figures. The purchaser was actually very smart, as his investment has returned a significant return from that monthly cash flow for the last several years. He bought himself a cash machine. I guess that's why he's a billionaire. He gets it!

Since most people do not have $1 million cash to invest, nor the ability to buy 10 homes, network marketing is *the* best way for anyone with no capital resources to live the lifestyle of cash flow like someone who has it. And best of all, anyone can build up their network marketing business on the side from their job. Again, like Jim Rohn taught, you work hard all day at your job earning a living, but you should work spare time, nights, and weekends building your fortune. So keep focused on that, and take that new income and multiply it by investing it properly.

My quick training point for you as you build your business is to treat every recruit as an asset. If you recruit someone but don't develop them into a productive distributor, they become a liability and not an asset. You merely wasted your time and money bringing them on board your team. Be sure that you help them become productive and earn an income, and you'll assure yourself a productive asset in your network. As a simple analogy, let's pretend you have 100 Coke machines placed all around town. If they are plugged in and the lights are on, people will stop and insert money for a soda. But if they are not plugged in, the machine can generate no revenue for you. The same goes with your distributors. Be sure to constantly check to make sure they are plugged in, and bringing in business.

The Fortune is in the Follow-up

I hope that you'll promise yourself — and me — that when you make it, you'll give back. That you'll become a difference maker. The money doesn't mean anything unless it means something to others. You don't want to have the identity of the rich person who only cares about his/her money pile and nobody else. What good would that be? You can't take it with you when you die. *Success* may be defined as creating personal wealth. *Significance* is making a difference and changing lives with your success.

The early part of my career was engulfed in chasing money and striving to amass a sizable bank account. I attached my identity to it. A person can feel a sense of importance the more money they have, because people will respect you more if you are successful. Maybe it's the desire for control, or maybe for security. Maybe you want to own nice things — homes, cars, boats, clothes, shoes, or jewelry. Please hear me: There is nothing wrong with any of this. I believe that if these things are inspirational, and they drive you to work harder and to become more, then great. But at the end of the day, if it was only about you and yours, you will feel a bit empty. The victory will be hollow.

After years of making money and accomplishing my personal goals, it dawned on me more and more that I was being drawn to be a positive factor in others' lives. I found it gratifying to use my success to help others. At first, I used my story to encourage others to help them in building their own businesses. Real, caring mentorship is not commonly found these days, and I enjoy pouring my heart, soul, time, and attention into

helping others achieve their own dreams. But then I also realized that I could not only afford to give away some of my
earnings — I felt an *obligation* to do so. It is not right for me
to hoard all of these blessings for myself. To whom much is
given, much is expected. I began paying it forward and trying
to make a difference by financially supporting charities that
touched my heart. *I discovered the joy in giving!*

Becoming a giver is hard if you are so used to being a taker.
Many of us are taught to go out into the world and stake our
claim. We have to work hard, day and night, to earn a living
to provide for ourselves. If we work hard enough, are smart
enough with our money, and follow a plan to put our money
away, some of us are blessed to build up a nest egg. To swallow
the idea of now giving it away is not easy to accept.

If not for a mentor in my life, the famous author and billionaire Paul J Meyer, I may not be a giver today. Paul taught me
the power in giving. I learned that when you give without the
intent of receiving anything in return, magic happens in your
life. The more you give, the more it comes back to you in a
multitude of ways. Paul shared with me that the more money
he gave away to his many charitable interests, the more his
own income kept increasing. He was trying intently to give his
money away as he was getting older before he died. But as his
giving increased, so did his income. He hired two accountants
to help him figure out how best to accomplish his goals of giv-

ing his money away faster and most effectively to do the greatest good. It was a predicament that I am sure every one of us would love to find happening to us!

Why not us?

The more we do for others, the more the universe has ways of repaying those good deeds. Before Paul passed away, he had personally given away over $400 million, and his Paul Meyer Foundation still continues to do good in the world ever since. Now that's the kind of legacy I want to leave behind. I want my life to mean something after I am gone. Don't you?

For the rest of us who are not able to give away $400 million, it all starts with adopting the same mindset and habits, and just operating in the same manner on a smaller scale at first. If we have agreed that the plan is to pay ourselves 10 percent first, and to give away 10 percent, and then to live off the remaining 80 percent, then that's the plan. Our giving will grow as our income grows. The 10 percent of a larger income will equate to larger giving. Plus, as our income surges, we will not need to spend all of this increase, so we can then increase the percentage of our income that we can give away. Isn't it exhilarating to think in this mindset of abundance rather than lack?

In the spirit of giving, and in the name of you, my readers, I am donating a portion of the proceeds from this book to helping put smiles onto the faces of kids who are fighting cancer (supporting www.SunshineKids.org) and to my local hospice (for families who are losing or have lost a family member). So please promote this book to your team. Not only will your team be more financially empowered because of you, you'll also be impacting these wonderful charitable causes.

Depending on the country in which you live, this may vary, but the U.S. government gives us incentives to donate to charities and non-profits in the form of tax breaks. Be sure to inquire with the entity to which you are giving money to ensure it is a true non-profit that qualifies for a tax deduction. You will be able to write off your charitable giving, taking the amount right off the top of your gross income, but as always, please seek counsel from your tax accountant for details.

Money. It's an interesting thing. We work very hard to get it. Then we are empowered to do impactful things with it. We must pursue the goal of being the master of money, and not let it master us. We see people every day doing bad things to get money. We see people with money using it in unscrupulous ways. Money is power. Money allows good people to do more good, and bad people to do more bad. So we need the good people to attract the money.

Here, at the end of this discussion around *money*, my hope is that you now view money and wealth in a different light. You should look at money as a source for good, and you should work on changing your relationship with money into a sort of love affair. Let yourself love what money is going to help you to do in this world, during and after your life. Work hard, attract money, pay your taxes (while keeping as much as you can), invest and grow your money, build wealth, become financially free, and become a perpetual giver so you can change the world.

Your Action List:

1. Open a separate *wealth* bank account and make your first deposit.
2. Decide and commit to paying yourself 10 percent first and set it up on automatic with your employer or bank.
3. Fill out your personal and business budget sheets.
4. Discuss this book with your family and get on the same page.
5. Discuss this book with your team and get them on the path toward wealth.

APPENDIX

This was my third book written to help the network marketing profession. My first, *Making My First Ten Million*, was a booklet published in 2013 as a recruiting tool. The short read is designed to open the door of receptivity in the minds of your prospects to want to learn about your leveraged income business opportunity. This book gets people into your business.

Discount Copies: www.MakingMyFirstTenMillion.com

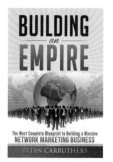

My second book, *Building an Empire*, was published in 2014. This was designed as the most complete training manual or blueprint on how to go from scratch to a seven-figure annual income in your network marketing business. The industry reviews have been incredible, and the book has been credited for a long list of people hitting the top positions in their respective companies. This book teaches you how to build your business.

Discount Copies: www.BuildinganEmpireBook.com

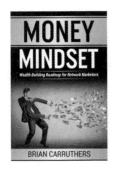

This latest book, *Money Mindset*, was the missing piece to the success puzzle. It's one thing to start a business, and another thing to make that business profitable. But what good is that successful business if you do not know how to keep and invest the money you are making? This book teaches you how to be smart with your money, and to grow your profits into your fortune.

Discount Copies: www.MLMmoneyBook.com

Please come visit my interactive blog and website for free training materials, videos, and mentorship. Get on my free mailing list for ongoing teaching and support. I am honored to play a small part in helping you achieve your ultimate success. www.FosterMentor.com